Mastering AutoCAD 2000